THE LONGMAN WRITER

RHETORIC AND READER